An Edition with Accompanying Study Notes
of the
Selected Poems of Christina Rossetti
for OCR A Level

Josephine Pearce

List of Rossetti Set Poems for OCR

SONG

When I am dead, my dearest,
  Sing no sad songs for me;
Plant thou no roses at my head,
  Nor shady cypress tree:
Be the green grass above me
  With showers and dewdrops wet;
And if thou wilt, remember,
  And if thou wilt, forget.

I shall not see the shadows,
  I shall not feel the rain;   10
I shall not hear the nightingale
  Sing on, as if in pain:
And dreaming through the twilight
  That doth not rise nor set,
Haply I may remember,
  And haply may forget.

SONG (1862)

ANALYSIS

The two stanzas are balanced and symmetrical to juxtapose the experience of death for those left behind and for the person who has died. The poem directly addresses the lover in the first stanza with affection. It is a series of imperatives, instructing the lover how to behave. The repetition of negatives emphasizes the speaker's dislike of traditional funeral rituals. No songs, roses or cypress trees – these are symbolic of exhibitionist grief, love, melancholy – which she does not want. She chooses green grass which is natural and eternal. It will always be watered by showers and dewdrops and will last forever – showers represent tears. The end of the first stanza ignores all the previous imperatives and offers the lover the choice of remembering or forgetting. There is no sense one is better than the other. The living must deal with death as they choose.

The second stanza is from the point of the view of the dead. It begins with more negatives, but this time it is the senses which no longer work for the dead person. They cannot see, feel or hear. However, the things they are unable to discern are all negative: shadows, rain and songs of pain. Does this mean that death is a better place? Death is imaged through the metaphor of a sleep. She is dreaming in a perpetual twilight. Dreaming sounds positive and the twilight suggests she is neither dead nor alive, but in a limbo.

The poem ends on the uncertainty of perhaps, "haply" – she is not sure what will happen – this is outside her control. Echoing the end of the first stanza which left the lover to determine their reaction, the dead speaker wonders if she will remember or forget. This suggests that her consciousness will continue after death and therefore she will be in the same position as her lover.

REMEMBER

Sonnet

Remember me when I am gone away,
  Gone far away into the silent land;
  When you can no more hold me by the hand,
Nor I half turn to go yet turning stay.
Remember me when no more day by day
  You tell me of our future that you planned:
  Only remember me; you understand
It will be late to counsel then or pray.
Yet if you should forget me for a while
  And afterwards remember, do not grieve:
  For if the darkness and corruption leave
  A vestige of the thoughts that once I had,
Better by far you should forget and smile
  Than that you should remember and be sad

Remember (1862)

ANALYSIS

It is a Petrarchan sonnet – a form which was normally employed by men to write love poems to women. Both the subject matter and the voice have been radically altered by the poet to create something startling. Instead of romantic love, the poem is about a great type of love beyond the physical and human which wants happiness for a loved one even when one cannot be with them. The fact the passion is expressed by a woman is equally startling for its time.

The poetic voice is authoritative and passionate, directly addressing the lover.

The octave is a series of repeated imperatives to "remember me" – this is directly addressed to the lover – we are eavesdropping. The repetition suggests that the voice is desperate to live on in the lover's mind; it possibly suggests that it is anxious that death will cancel the love out.

The repetition of "gone away" suggests the vastness of death – death is a long journey removing her from her lover.

Death is imaged as a "silent land" – this metaphor creates a sense of death and the afterlife as a lonely and remote place where she will hear no one.

This contrasts with her life with her lover – it will be a time when he can no longer hold her hand. This image suggests physical affection, but also a sense of restraint. He is battling against death and trying to keep her, but this won't work.

She is also unable to control her own death – she will be unable to decide if she wants to stay – there is a sense of death removing her authority which she tries hard to reassert through the poem which is repetitive and imperative. These devices then come to show insecurity rather than confidence

The volta in line 8 changes the direction of the sonnet. The final sestet begins with "Yet", showing that she is hesitant. She runs on rapidly in the sestet with enjambment, creating one long sentence. It is as if the final sentiment is overwhelming and has to be expressed rapidly. She thinks about what will happen when he forgets her for a while and wants him not to feel bad about this inevitable moving on. She would rather he forgot her and lived a happy life, than remembered her and was sad after she is gone.

Death is imaged more actively in the sestet. Instead of being a distant land, it is a place of "darkness and corruption". This suggests something sinister and decaying. It is frightening.

The "vestige of the thoughts" suggests that she hopes even in the horror of death a part of her consciousness will stay and will realise that his happiness is more important than her desire for him to remember her. It becomes a self-sacrificing sentiment. The title "Remember" is therefore ironic, as by the end of the poem she knows that the kindest thing she could hope for her lover is that he will forget her and move on with his life.

FROM THE ANTIQUE (IT'S A WEARY LIFE, IT IS, SHE SAID)

It's a weary life, it is, she said:
Doubly blank in a woman's lot:
I wish and I wish I were a man:
Or, better then any being, were not:

Were nothing at all in all the world,
Not a body and not a soul:
Not so much as a grain of dust
Or a drop of water from pole to pole.

Still the world would wag on the same,
Still the seasons go and come:
Blossoms bloom as in days of old,
Cherries ripen and wild bees hum.

None would miss me in all the world,
How much less would care or weep:
I should be nothing, while all the rest
Would wake and weary and fall asleep.

FROM THE ANTIQUE (IT'S A WEARY LIFE, IT IS, SHE SAID)

ANALYSIS

The poem is in four stanzas which begin and end with the weariness of life. This suggests that living has no meaning and is just hard and tiring. There is the sense the character cannot escape this thought as their ideas never progress beyond it.

It is not the poet speaking, but a character – a woman with no name. Why is she denied a name? Does she represent all women or is she so insignificant in the world that she does not deserve a name? The speaker speaks the whole of the rest of the poem which is left there as a pronouncement for us to judge and consider. It is not the poet's thought, but a character created by her telling us an opinion which must be contemplated.

Life is described as weary, but "doubly blank" for a woman. This image makes life seem twice as bad for a woman. However, it is not just wearying for women. It is blank. This implies that it is entirely empty. The life of a woman must be without meaning or worth.

Repetitions throughout suggest a sense of desperation and exhaustion and a desire for something better. The repetition of "wish" elicits a feeling of a fairy tale, but this wish is to become another gender – she wants to be a man. What would this represent for her? Perhaps it would represent a lack of blankness – an ability to do something worthwhile?

But even men would be better not being alive as life is so tiring – "were not" – is a euphemism for death? Or the suggestion that people should just not exist in the world?

The second stanza imagines a world with no people – neither physically nor spiritually. She uses images of vastness to illustrate – "a grain of dust" is tiny and a drop of water from pole to pole suggests the expanse of the world in which there is nothing human.

In stanza three the repetition of "still" shows that the character knows the world would carry on. The verb "wag" suggests the world would go on without the weariness of human life. "wag" makes it sound easy and light hearted. Indeed nature without people seems really positive with seasons and blossoms and cherries and bees. It remains a more beautiful world without people.

Finally the woman says no one would miss her and there would not be any grief expressed for her loss. In this case she concludes it would be better – she "should" be nothing – but the rest of humanity should carry on living as she is so unimportant. The description of the cycle of life is habitual and negative. Life is imagined as one day in which people wake, grow tired and sleep. It is all just a process of exhaustion which nature is not a part of. It seems to be manmade.

The poem is an insight into a character without a spiritual belief. Does it suggest that life without Christianity is "blank"?

ECHO

Come to me in the silence of the night;
  Come in the speaking silence of a dream;
Come with soft rounded cheeks and eyes as bright
  As sunlight on a stream;
    Come back in tears,
O memory, hope, love of finished years.

Oh dream how sweet, too sweet, too bitter sweet,
  Whose wakening should have been in Paradise,
Where souls brimfull of love abide and meet;
  Where thirsting longing eyes   10
    Watch the slow door
That opening, letting in, lets out no more.

Yet come to me in dreams, that I may live
  My very life again though cold in death:
Come back to me in dreams, that I may give
  Pulse for pulse, breath for breath:
    Speak low, lean low,
As long ago, my love, how long ago!

ECHO

ANALYSIS

The title suggests a sound memory. This is a poem about communicating with something which is now in the past or dead. The poem describes how she can communicate with her dead lover while she is dreaming. The echo is the sound he has left for her.

The first stanza is full of urgency. She repeatedly begs him to "Come to me". Although it is an instruction, it sounds desperate rather than authoritative because of the repetition.

She begs him to come in the silence of the night – but this is ironic – as it is when it is apparently quiet that she is able to hear him and communicate with him. This paradox is highlighted in the oxymoronic image of the "speaking silence" of a dream. The dream is able to communicate with her although it is quiet and no one else can hear it.

The way she imagines her dead lover with rounded cheeks and bright eyes suggests that in the dream he is not dead or sick, but looking healthy and alive. She uses the simile of his eyes as bright "as sunlight on a stream". The image suggests daytime and life which are the opposite of what he now is.

The "O" is an exclamation of extreme emotion. She is desperate.

She wants him to come back even if it causes sadness – tears – she wants the love of the time which is now over or "finished".

The second stanza begins with more emotion – "Oh" – but this time she is happy because she is in the dream world which brings him to life. The dream is sweet but the repeated "too" suggests that the fantasy is so good it is damaging. The oxymoron of "bitter sweet" shows the confusion of emotions. When she wakes from sleep, she is no longer in "Paradise". Paradise seems to be both being with her lover and death, as that would bring the two of them back together. It is the place where their souls can live and meet.

She imagines in the place where her dead lover is her "thirsting longing eyes" – they are hungry and full of desire for him. She is describing immense passion and desire.

The eyes watch a "slow door" – which is a symbol of the barrier between their two worlds. It is an obstacle to their communication, as well as an entry point for her to reach him. The door is opening – because it is death - and letting people in – but it can never let them leave. She is watching at the door for him, but she cannot yet enter.

The final stanza begins with "Yet" or however – she is brought back to reality. She still wants him to come to her in dreams so she can live her life over again even though it is actually dead.

If he comes back in dreams she can be equal to him. Her description of their meeting is sensual and passionate. She meets him with her pulse, breath and speech, remembering how they were long ago. But her dream crumbles in the truth of reality and she exclaims "how long ago!" their intimacy now was. Her dream has not succeeded in reviving him – it has just reminded her of how much time has passed since they were together.

SHUT OUT

The door was shut. I looked between
  Its iron bars; and saw it lie,
  My garden, mine, beneath the sky,
Pied with all flowers bedewed and green:

From bough to bough the song-birds crossed,
  From flower to flower the moths and bees;
  With all its nests and stately trees
It had been mine, and it was lost.

A shadowless spirit kept the gate,
  Blank and unchanging like the grave.   10
  I peering through said: 'Let me have
Some buds to cheer my outcast state.'

He answered not. 'Or give me, then,
  But one small twig from shrub or tree;
  And bid my home remember me
Until I come to it again.'

The spirit was silent; but he took
  Mortar and stone to build a wall;
  He left no loophole great or small
Through which my straining eyes might look: 20

So now I sit here quite alone
  Blinded with tears; nor grieve for that,
  For nought is left worth looking at
Since my delightful land is gone.

A violet bed is budding near,
  Wherein a lark has made her nest:
  And good they are, but not the best;
And dear they are, but not so dear.

SHUT OUT

ANALYSIS

The seven stanzas have a regular rhyme scheme of ABBA. The regular rhythm and rhyme belies the agitation of the poetic voice's experience.

The poem opens with the door shut, but the title tells us she is Shut Out. This suggests she is trapped outside somewhere she wants to enter. It forces the reader to reassess ideas of entrapment and imprisonment – one can be trapped outside something when one is actually free.

The door has iron bars which allow her to peep in. The iron is symbolic of something hard and impenetrable. The garden is not to be accessed easily. The fact she sees it "lie" in front of her suggests double meanings of deceit and openness. Repetition of possessive pronouns "my" and "mine" remind the reader that what she looks at was once hers. She has lost her home. The description of the garden "pied" with flowers suggests it is dappled with many different colours. The "bedewed" is both natural, but also reminiscent of bejewelled. Therefore the garden is both precious and natural.

She describes the garden with song birds, flowers and nests. The items are both delightful to hear and see. The moths and bees suggest both productivity and mortality working together. They represent the day and night working simultaneously. This means the garden must have eliminated time and decay. It is beyond mortality; it is paradise. The garden was hers but has been lost.

The sibilance of "shadowless spirit" conjures up the idea of something without substance and existence. It exists without the sun or time. This is important in a poem about sight. The spirit is constant; described using the simile "like the grave". It is permanent and unbending. She begs it first for buds which suggest new life and then for a twig. She wants an item to remind her of home, but more importantly to make the garden remember her and wait for her to come again. She is hopeful that she can return to it in the future.

The spirit silently denies her, building a wall. This is a permanent barrier, unlike the door. It also will not allow her to see paradise. Left alone, she cries until she can't see, but this is of no matter as there is nothing worth looking at.

She notices a violet bed and a lark. Violets represent faithfulness. Does this mean she will be loyal to her vision of paradise and persist in working towards it? The lark represents hope and life. They are both dear and good, but they are not the best. They are pale versions of the perfect Platonic image of paradise which she must settle for now.

IN THE ROUND TOWER AT JHANSI

June 8, 1857

A hundred, a thousand to one; even so;
  Not a hope in the world remained:
The swarming howling wretches below
  Gained and gained and gained.

Skene looked at his pale young wife:—
  'Is the time come?'—'The time is come!'—
Young, strong, and so full of life:
  The agony struck them dumb.

Close his arm about her now,
  Close her cheek to his,   10
Close the pistol to her brow—
  God forgive them this!

'Will it hurt much?'—'No, mine own:
  I wish I could bear the pang for both.'
'I wish I could bear the pang alone:
  Courage, dear, I am not loth.'

Kiss and kiss: 'It is not pain
  Thus to kiss and die.
One kiss more.'—'And yet one again.'—
  'Good-bye.'—'Good-bye.'   20

IN THE ROUND TOWER AT JHANSI JUNE 8, 1857 (PUBLISHED 1862)

ANALYSIS

The poem is based on historical events reported during the Indian Rebellion of 1857, although Rossetti wrote a footnote for the poem in 1875 explaining that it had subsequently been revealed that the Skene family did not commit suicide, but were captured and killed.

It is a dramatic poem with five stanzas of regular rhythm and rhyme scheme – ABAB. The regularity highlights the horror of the events described. The voices of the couple are dramatized and hearing them speak makes the events seem immediate and urgent. The relationship between the couple is powerfully rendered. Their love and bravery is described.

The opening stanza suggests there are lots of Indians attacking them and there is no hope. The loss of hope is underlined by the description of the rebels who are dehumanised. They are "swarming" like bees and "howling" like wolves. These metaphors suggest the number and savagery of the rebels. The repetition of "gained" shows that the rebels are relentless and inevitable. The poem presents traditional racial stereotypes.

Now we are introduced to the key characters, Skene and his wife. She is pale due to fear. She is left without a name; her only significance is as an appendage of her husband. They have clearly already planned their suicide pact as she asks if the time has come. Skene takes charge and tells her it has. It is a very traditional picture of patriarchal authority. It revels in the stereotypes of masculine authority and female submission and obedience. We are given their dialogue to make them more real and immediate. In response to her question of how much it will hurt, he replies that he wishes he could take the burden from her. However, she then replies saying "I wish I could bear the pang alone". This produces the stereotype of the Victorian brave wife. Moreover, she then goes on to encourage her husband to be brave: "Courage, dear". She is very much a brave partner and one who is active in their choice of suicide. The description of their actions repeats the word "Close" first to describe physical intimacy and love, and then to describe Skene raising a pistol to his wife's head. The reader is given a shocking contrast between the closeness of love and suicide. The poetic voice erupts with an exclamation "God forgive them this!" to show the opprobrium heaped on suicide, but in this case it is presented as brave.

They end kissing each other and saying goodbye just before the moment of the gun shots. The dialogue in this stanza does not clearly delineate which person is speaking. This suggests that at the end they are so united that their voices are indistinguishable.

The reader is left to admire their love and bravery.

A BIRTHDAY

My heart is like a singing bird
  Whose nest is in a watered shoot;
My heart is like an apple-tree
  Whose boughs are bent with thickset fruit;
My heart is like a rainbow shell
  That paddles in a halcyon sea;
My heart is gladder than all these
  Because my love is come to me.

Raise me a dais of silk and down;
  Hang it with vair and purple dyes;   10
Carve it in doves, and pomegranates,
  And peacocks with a hundred eyes;
Work it in gold and silver grapes,
  In leaves, and silver fleurs-de-lys;
Because the birthday of my life
  Is come, my love is come to me.

A BIRTHDAY (1861)

ANALYSIS

The poem is divided into two eight line stanzas each with an irregular rhyme scheme.

The poem is spoken by someone who has found an intense and perfect love which they want to celebrate. The poem says that the true day a person is born is the day when they meet the person they love. This is when they really come to life. This love could be for a lover or for Christ. The images suggest spring time and could refer to Easter and Jesus's resurrection.

The first stanza is a series of repetitions of "My heart is like" each simile attempts to describe perfect love. However, the fact that she keeps adding more new images suggests that each one is inadequate in describing the beauty and passion which she feels. The poem seems to say that words are unable to express perfect love. The similes are all natural. Her joy is like a singing bird, an apple tree full of fruit and a rainbow shell. The images span different types of nature. They include different senses of hearing and sight, as well as ideas of abundance and nourishment. However, by the end of the stanza she has not yet explained how glad she is as her heart is more happy than all these because her love has come.

The second stanza moves to manmade, high status images which are the opposite of the first stanza. Here she describes a birthday feast to celebrate her love which is full of precious objects. There is a dais or altar covered in silk and "vair" which is squirrel fur. The purple dyes suggest something royal. The doves represent peace and the pomegranates are a symbol of love in the Persephone myth, and also of rarity and exoticism. The peacocks, gold and silver are also rare commodities. Finally the fleurs de lys represent the French royal family and are again part of a weaving of majestic and precious images to describe the feast which her love deserves. The poem concludes with an explanation. This must happen "Because" her life has only just begun because she has now found love.

MAUDE CLARE

Out of the church she followed them
  With a lofty step and mien:
His bride was like a village maid,
  Maude Clare was like a queen.

'Son Thomas,' his lady mother said,
  With smiles, almost with tears:
'May Nell and you but live as true
  As we have done for years;

'Your father thirty years ago
  Had just your tale to tell;   10
But he was not so pale as you,
  Nor I so pale as Nell.'

My lord was pale with inward strife,
  And Nell was pale with pride;
My lord gazed long on pale Maude Clare
  Or ever he kissed the bride.

'Lo, I have brought my gift, my lord,
  Have brought my gift,' she said:
'To bless the hearth, to bless the board,
  To bless the marriage-bed.   20

'Here's my half of the golden chain
  You wore about your neck,
That day we waded ankle-deep
  For lilies in the beck:

'Here's my half of the faded leaves
  We plucked from budding bough,
With feet amongst the lily leaves,—
  The lilies are budding now.'

He strove to match her scorn with scorn,
  He faltered in his place: 30
'Lady,' he said,—'Maude Clare,' he said,—
  'Maude Clare:'—and hid his face.

She turn'd to Nell: 'My Lady Nell,
  I have a gift for you;

Though, were it fruit, the bloom were gone,
  Or, were it flowers, the dew.

'Take my share of a fickle heart,
  Mine of a paltry love:
Take it or leave it as you will,
  I wash my hands thereof.'   40

'And what you leave,' said Nell, 'I'll take,
  And what you spurn, I'll wear;
For he's my lord for better and worse,
  And him I love, Maude Clare.

'Yea, though you're taller by the head,
  More wise, and much more fair;
I'll love him till he loves me best,
  Me best of all, Maude Clare.'

MAUDE CLARE

ANALYSIS

The poem is written in the ballad form with 12 stanzas of four lines. However, instead of the typical ballad rhyme scheme of ABAB, Rossetti employs ABCB which makes it seem more awkward and full of tension.

The poem dwells on the idea that marriage is not an ideal of fulfilled love.

After the wedding ceremony, Maude Clare interrupts the bride and groom. She is like a queen – showing her indignation makes her majestic, while Nell's diffidence reduces her to the level of a village maid.

The pre-existing relationship does not seem to have been disguised as Sir Thomas's own mother knows the situation and advises him on it. This shows that such behaviour is common and that ideals of married love are false or questionable. The mother tells them not to worry as the same thing happened to her husband thirty years ago. Clearly marriage has always been blighted by other lovers.

Nell and Sir Thomas are pale at this suggestion and seem not to take it well. Sir Thomas is pale from turbulent emotion, while Nell is pale from embarrassment.

Maude Clare presents them with gifts. This is appropriate for a wedding, but she does it not to celebrate, but to humiliate. She offers Sir Thomas the half of the chain he gave her and the leaves they collected together. Each item suggests that they were whole only when together. The chain symbolically suggests they have also been bound together, but not in a marriage ceremony. Their intercourse has been in nature with naked feet in a stream plucking lilies. The image is sexual and informal, showing they have been intimate outside marriage. Lilies normally represent purity with the Virgin Mary and the annunciation. Do they suggest here that the love was pure and true? Do they suggest that like Mary, Maude is also pregnant? The leaves are an image of decay, showing something which has not lasted. The lilies are budding now so there is new life.

Sir Thomas tries to match Maude's emotion but his words are faltering. His lines have a caesura to show he breaks off and cannot speak to her. Is this due to guilt or love? He also does not know what to call her, switching between lady and Maude Clare. He hides his face, showing shame.

Then she offers Nell Sir Thomas's fickle heart and meagre love. Nell responds with dignity. She takes what is left and says he is her lord for better and worse, echoing the marriage ceremony. She does not scorn her husband, but accepts and loves him. Her restraint is a stereotype of the good Victorian wife. She says her love and persistence will mean in the future he will love her more than Maude.

The women are polar opposites of each other – a scorned, outraged woman full of anger and expressing her sexual indignation even though this removes her from polite society – and the good wife who is restrained emotionally and simply abides by her vows. Rossetti does not say which woman she admires most, but the poem is entitled Maude Clare.

UP-HILL

Does the road wind up-hill all the way?
  Yes, to the very end.
Will the day's journey take the whole long day?
  From morn to night, my friend.

But is there for the night a resting-place?
  A roof for when the slow dark hours begin.
May not the darkness hide it from my face?
  You cannot miss that inn.

Shall I meet other wayfarers at night?
  Those who have gone before. 10
Then must I knock, or call when just in sight?
  They will not keep you standing at that door.

Shall I find comfort, travel-sore and weak?
  Of labour you shall find the sum.
Will there be beds for me and all who seek?
  Yea, beds for all who come.

UP HILL

ANALYSIS

The poem consists of 8 questions and answers. This structure is typical in devotional verse as it gives the reader the opportunity to contemplate their own answer to the questions. The regular rhyme scheme of ABAB means each speaker is given a different rhyme to separate their voices. The consistent pace of the lines mimics the pace of the journey up hill.

Each question is posed by a traveller to a guide. The guide addresses the traveller as "my friend" – this is what Jesus called his disciples.

The poem consists of an extended metaphor of the journey. The journey seems to be of life which is up hill and therefore consistently hard until one gets to the top. The question is whether or not the inn at the top is death or heaven. Is the traveller to experience some respite from the arduous journey?

The traveller is concerned that they must travel all day until there is no light. The darkness could represent death or troubles in life. The guide reassures them that even in the dark there is an inn which can be seen. They are reassured that they will meet other wayfarers who have gone before. The suggestion that they must knock or call intimates that each person must look for or seek out comfort. This could be Christian confession of sin to gain admittance to heaven. The traveller is reassured that there is comfort and respite at the inn, so there will be an end to arduous endeavour. This could be heaven where there is no more toiling up hill and others there to be companions.

'NO, THANK YOU, JOHN'

I never said I loved you, John:
  Why will you tease me day by day,
And wax a weariness to think upon
  With always 'do' and 'pray'?

You know I never loved you, John;
  No fault of mine made me your toast:
Why will you haunt me with a face as wan
  As shows an hour-old ghost?

I dare say Meg or Moll would take
  Pity upon you, if you'd ask: 10
And pray don't remain single for my sake
  Who can't perform that task.

I have no heart?—Perhaps I have not;
  But then you're mad to take offence
That I don't give you what I have not got:
  Use your own common sense.

Let bygones be bygones:
  Don't call me false, who owed not to be true:
I'd rather answer 'No' to fifty Johns
  Than answer 'Yes' to you.   20

Let's mar our pleasant days no more,
  Song-birds of passage, days of youth:
Catch at to-day, forget the days before:
  I'll wink at your untruth.

Let us strike hands as hearty friends;
  No more, no less; and friendship's good:
Only don't keep in view ulterior ends,
  And points not understood

In open treaty. Rise above
  Quibbles and shuffling off and on: 30
Here's friendship for you if you like; but love,—
  No, thank you, John.

NO, THANK YOU, JOHN

ANALYSIS

The poem is written as a dramatic monologue with an unnamed woman turning down John's proposal of marriage. The woman's character is remarkable in its frankness, sense of equality with the man and desire not to marry him. John's voice is only heard through the responses of the speaker. He is silenced so only her voice dominates. Is she simply a remarkably forthright woman of her day or is she a prostitute who has beguiled a customer who has become tiresome? The fact it seems so odd for a woman to reject a loving man shows how society expects women to want male admiration.

The first two stanzas are questions wondering at why he keeps teasing her with begging. She wonders why he haunts her like a ghost. John is depicted as subservient and also sick with love. He looks wan or pale like a ghost newly dead. Love has made him unwell.

She says she cannot marry him and that he should not remain single. She suggests the names of other women who would take pity on him. This makes John seem vulnerable and weak. His masculine power is removed by the speaker's apparent efforts to console him.

John suggests she has no heart outside the lines of the poem and she replies that if that is the case he is foolish to expect her to return his love. Her logic is cold and implacable. She reasons with him like a stereotypical man, while his behaviour is more typically female - full of emotion and pleading.

She finally suggests in a masculine way that they should call a truce. This diction is military and masculine, suggesting a meeting of equals which would not be typical between the sexes. She recommends he seize the happiness of today and she'll turn a blind eye to what he's said about love. This offers to save his pride.

Her suggestion they should "strike hands" is again quite masculine. She wants an equal friendship which does not expect ulterior ends. This means she is not playing games and is speaking frankly and openly to him. This is again untypical of female characters. She finally offers friendship but not love. Her denial is polite with no "thank you". Her good manners suggest she is courteous and has simply chosen a different sort of female life.

GOOD FRIDAY

Am I a stone and not a sheep
  That I can stand, O Christ, beneath Thy Cross,
  To number drop by drop Thy Blood's slow loss,
And yet not weep?

Not so those women loved
  Who with exceeding grief lamented Thee;
  Not so fallen Peter weeping bitterly;
Not so the thief was moved;

Not so the Sun and Moon
  Which hid their faces in a starless sky,   10
  A horror of great darkness at broad noon—
I, only I.

Yet give not o'er,
  But seek Thy sheep, true Shepherd of the flock;
  Greater than Moses, turn and look once more
And smite a rock.

GOOD FRIDAY

ANALYSIS

A deeply personal poem addressed to Christ on Good Friday which reimagines the crucifixion happening now. She sees Christ bleeding to death on the cross, but she is appalled by the fact she cannot weep for him.

She asks if she is a stone or a sheep. A stone is a metaphor for an emotionless, unchristian person who cannot respond to Jesus. It also alludes to the Greek word for Peter which means rock. Jesus said he was his rock. A sheep suggests someone who is part of Jesus's flock already.

Her description of the crucifixion is poignant. Christ is slowly bleeding to death in front of her. She sees the drops of blood.

Then she remembers all the people and things which were moved to tears by Jesus's crucifixion. She emphasizes how many of these there were by repeating the words "Not so" at the beginning of each line to underline that others reacted differently to her. The women who loved Jesus are his mother and Mary Magdalene who were both present at the crucifixion. Peter is one of the disciples who also wept, while a thief being crucified next to Jesus was moved by his plight. Jesus predicted that Peter would deny him thrice before the cock crowed on the day of his crucifixion. Peter did this. He then went on to found the Catholic Church in Rome and was crucified himself upside down because he said he did not deserve to die in the same way as Christ. Even more astonishingly, the sun and moon are personified hiding their faces from the sight of Jesus's death by creating an eclipse in the middle of the day when Christ died. The third stanza ends with "I, only I" to show she is the only person who is unmoved by Jesus's sacrifice.

The final stanza brings hope. She begs to Christ that he should seek her out. She alludes to the Exodus story of Moses. After taking the Jews from Egypt, they were complaining of thirst and Moses asked God what to do. God told him to strike a stone with his staff and when he did so, it erupted with water and quenched all the Israelites. The speaker says Jesus is greater than Moses and just needs to strike the rock or her and then she will erupt with water or emotion and be able to feel moved by his crucifixion.

The poem ends with hope, but it remains dependent on Christ coming to get her.

GOBLIN MARKET

Morning and evening
Maids heard the goblins cry:
'Come buy our orchard fruits,
Come buy, come buy:
Apples and quinces,
Lemons and oranges,
Plump unpecked cherries,
Melons and raspberries,
Bloom-down-cheeked peaches,
Swart-headed mulberries,   10
Wild free-born cranberries,
Crab-apples, dewberries,
Pine-apples, blackberries,
Apricots, strawberries;—
All ripe together
In summer weather,—
Morns that pass by,
Fair eves that fly;
Come buy, come buy:
Our grapes fresh from the vine,   20
Pomegranates full and fine,
Dates and sharp bullaces,
Rare pears and greengages,
Damsons and bilberries,
Taste them and try:
Currants and gooseberries,
Bright-fire-like barberries,
Figs to fill your mouth,
Citrons from the South,
Sweet to tongue and sound to eye;   30
Come buy, come buy.'

  Evening by evening
Among the brookside rushes,
Laura bowed her head to hear,
Lizzie veiled her blushes:
Crouching close together
In the cooling weather,
With clasping arms and cautioning lips,
With tingling cheeks and finger tips.
'Lie close,' Laura said,   40
Pricking up her golden head:
'We must not look at goblin men,
We must not buy their fruits:

Who knows upon what soil they fed
Their hungry thirsty roots?'
'Come buy,' call the goblins
Hobbling down the glen.
'Oh,' cried Lizzie, 'Laura, Laura,
You should not peep at goblin men.'
Lizzie covered up her eyes,   50
Covered close lest they should look;
Laura reared her glossy head,
And whispered like the restless brook:
'Look, Lizzie, look, Lizzie,
Down the glen tramp little men.
One hauls a basket,
One bears a plate,
One lugs a golden dish
Of many pounds weight.
How fair the vine must grow   60
Whose grapes are so luscious;
How warm the wind must blow
Through those fruit bushes.'
'No,' said Lizzie, 'No, no, no;
Their offers should not charm us,
Their evil gifts would harm us.'
She thrust a dimpled finger
In each ear, shut eyes and ran:
Curious Laura chose to linger
Wondering at each merchant man.   70
One had a cat's face,
One whisked a tail,
One tramped at a rat's pace,
One crawled like a snail,
One like a wombat prowled obtuse and furry,
One like a ratel tumbled hurry skurry.
She heard a voice like voice of doves
Cooing all together:
They sounded kind and full of loves
In the pleasant weather.   80

   Laura stretched her gleaming neck
Like a rush-imbedded swan,
Like a lily from the beck,
Like a moonlit poplar branch,
Like a vessel at the launch
When its last restraint is gone.

   Backwards up the mossy glen
Turned and trooped the goblin men,
With their shrill repeated cry,

'Come buy, come buy.'   90
When they reached where Laura was
They stood stock still upon the moss,
Leering at each other,
Brother with queer brother;
Signalling each other,
Brother with sly brother.
One set his basket down,
One reared his plate;
One began to weave a crown
Of tendrils, leaves, and rough nuts brown   100
(Men sell not such in any town);
One heaved the golden weight
Of dish and fruit to offer her:
'Come buy, come buy,' was still their cry.
Laura stared but did not stir,
Longed but had no money:
The whisk-tailed merchant bade her taste
In tones as smooth as honey,
The cat-faced purr'd,
The rat-faced spoke a word   110
Of welcome, and the snail-paced even was heard;
One parrot-voiced and jolly
Cried 'Pretty Goblin' still for 'Pretty Polly;'—
One whistled like a bird.

  But sweet-tooth Laura spoke in haste:
'Good folk, I have no coin;
To take were to purloin:
I have no copper in my purse,
I have no silver either,
And all my gold is on the furze   120
That shakes in windy weather
Above the rusty heather.'
'You have much gold upon your head,'
They answered all together:
'Buy from us with a golden curl.'
She clipped a precious golden lock,
She dropped a tear more rare than pearl,
Then sucked their fruit globes fair or red:
Sweeter than honey from the rock,
Stronger than man-rejoicing wine,   130
Clearer than water flowed that juice;
She never tasted such before,
How should it cloy with length of use?
She sucked and sucked and sucked the more
Fruits which that unknown orchard bore;
She sucked until her lips were sore;

Then flung the emptied rinds away
But gathered up one kernel stone,
And knew not was it night or day
As she turned home alone.   140

   Lizzie met her at the gate
Full of wise upbraidings:
'Dear, you should not stay so late,
Twilight is not good for maidens;
Should not loiter in the glen
In the haunts of goblin men.
Do you not remember Jeanie,
How she met them in the moonlight,
Took their gifts both choice and many,
Ate their fruits and wore their flowers   150
Plucked from bowers
Where summer ripens at all hours?
But ever in the noonlight
She pined and pined away;
Sought them by night and day,
Found them no more, but dwindled and grew grey;
Then fell with the first snow,
While to this day no grass will grow
Where she lies low:
I planted daisies there a year ago   160
That never blow.
You should not loiter so.'
'Nay, hush,' said Laura:
'Nay, hush, my sister:
I ate and ate my fill,
Yet my mouth waters still;
To-morrow night I will
Buy more:' and kissed her:
'Have done with sorrow;
I'll bring you plums to-morrow   170
Fresh on their mother twigs,
Cherries worth getting;
You cannot think what figs
My teeth have met in,
What melons icy-cold
Piled on a dish of gold
Too huge for me to hold,
What peaches with a velvet nap,
Pellucid grapes without one seed:
Odorous indeed must be the mead   180
Whereon they grow, and pure the wave they drink
With lilies at the brink,
And sugar-sweet their sap.'

Golden head by golden head,
Like two pigeons in one nest
Folded in each other's wings,
They lay down in their curtained bed:
Like two blossoms on one stem,
Like two flakes of new-fall'n snow,
Like two wands of ivory   190
Tipped with gold for awful kings.
Moon and stars gazed in at them,
Wind sang to them lullaby,
Lumbering owls forbore to fly,
Not a bat flapped to and fro
Round their rest:
Cheek to cheek and breast to breast
Locked together in one nest.

Early in the morning
When the first cock crowed his warning,   200
Neat like bees, as sweet and busy,
Laura rose with Lizzie:
Fetched in honey, milked the cows,
Aired and set to rights the house,
Kneaded cakes of whitest wheat,
Cakes for dainty mouths to eat,
Next churned butter, whipped up cream,
Fed their poultry, sat and sewed;
Talked as modest maidens should:
Lizzie with an open heart,   210
Laura in an absent dream,
One content, one sick in part;
One warbling for the mere bright day's delight,
One longing for the night.

At length slow evening came:
They went with pitchers to the reedy brook;
Lizzie most placid in her look,
Laura most like a leaping flame.
They drew the gurgling water from its deep;
Lizzie plucked purple and rich golden flags,   220
Then turning homeward said: 'The sunset flushes
Those furthest loftiest crags;
Come, Laura, not another maiden lags,
No wilful squirrel wags,
The beasts and birds are fast asleep.'
But Laura loitered still among the rushes
And said the bank was steep.

And said the hour was early still
The dew not fall'n, the wind not chill:
Listening ever, but not catching   230
The customary cry,
'Come buy, come buy,'
With its iterated jingle
Of sugar-baited words:
Not for all her watching
Once discerning even one goblin
Racing, whisking, tumbling, hobbling;
Let alone the herds
That used to tramp along the glen,
In groups or single,   240
Of brisk fruit-merchant men.

    Till Lizzie urged, 'O Laura, come;
I hear the fruit-call but I dare not look:
You should not loiter longer at this brook:
Come with me home.
The stars rise, the moon bends her arc,
Each glowworm winks her spark,
Let us get home before the night grows dark:
For clouds may gather
Though this is summer weather,   250
Put out the lights and drench us through;
Then if we lost our way what should we do?'

    Laura turned cold as stone
To find her sister heard that cry alone,
That goblin cry,
'Come buy our fruits, come buy.'
Must she then buy no more such dainty fruit?
Must she no more such succous pasture find,
Gone deaf and blind?
Her tree of life drooped from the root: 260
She said not one word in her heart's sore ache;
But peering thro' the dimness, nought discerning,
Trudged home, her pitcher dripping all the way;
So crept to bed, and lay
Silent till Lizzie slept;
Then sat up in a passionate yearning,
And gnashed her teeth for baulked desire, and wept
As if her heart would break.

    Day after day, night after night,
Laura kept watch in vain   270
In sullen silence of exceeding pain.
She never caught again the goblin cry:

'Come buy, come buy;'—
She never spied the goblin men
Hawking their fruits along the glen:
But when the noon waxed bright
Her hair grew thin and grey;
She dwindled, as the fair full moon doth turn
To swift decay and burn
Her fire away.   280

   One day remembering her kernel-stone
She set it by a wall that faced the south;
Dewed it with tears, hoped for a root,
Watched for a waxing shoot,
But there came none;
It never saw the sun,
It never felt the trickling moisture run:
While with sunk eyes and faded mouth
She dreamed of melons, as a traveller sees
False waves in desert drouth   290
With shade of leaf-crowned trees,
And burns the thirstier in the sandful breeze.

   She no more swept the house,
Tended the fowls or cows,
Fetched honey, kneaded cakes of wheat,
Brought water from the brook:
But sat down listless in the chimney-nook
And would not eat.

   Tender Lizzie could not bear
To watch her sister's cankerous care   300
Yet not to share.
She night and morning
Caught the goblins' cry:
'Come buy our orchard fruits,
Come buy, come buy:'—
Beside the brook, along the glen,
She heard the tramp of goblin men,
The voice and stir
Poor Laura could not hear;
Longed to buy fruit to comfort her,   310
But feared to pay too dear.
She thought of Jeanie in her grave,
Who should have been a bride;
But who for joys brides hope to have
Fell sick and died
In her gay prime,
In earliest Winter time

With the first glazing rime,
With the first snow-fall of crisp Winter time.

  Till Laura dwindling   320
Seemed knocking at Death's door:
Then Lizzie weighed no more
Better and worse;
But put a silver penny in her purse,
Kissed Laura, crossed the heath with clumps of furze
At twilight, halted by the brook:
And for the first time in her life
Began to listen and look.

  Laughed every goblin
When they spied her peeping: 330
Came towards her hobbling,
Flying, running, leaping,
Puffing and blowing,
Chuckling, clapping, crowing,
Clucking and gobbling,
Mopping and mowing,
Full of airs and graces,
Pulling wry faces,
Demure grimaces,
Cat-like and rat-like,   340
Ratel- and wombat-like,
Snail-paced in a hurry,
Parrot-voiced and whistler,
Helter skelter, hurry skurry,
Chattering like magpies,
Fluttering like pigeons,
Gliding like fishes,—
Hugged her and kissed her:
Squeezed and caressed her:
Stretched up their dishes,   350
Panniers, and plates:
'Look at our apples
Russet and dun,
Bob at our cherries,
Bite at our peaches,
Citrons and dates,
Grapes for the asking,
Pears red with basking
Out in the sun,
Plums on their twigs;   360
Pluck them and suck them,
Pomegranates, figs.'—

'Good folk,' said Lizzie,
Mindful of Jeanie:
'Give me much and many:'—
Held out her apron,
Tossed them her penny.
'Nay, take a seat with us,
Honour and eat with us,'
They answered grinning: 370
'Our feast is but beginning.
Night yet is early,
Warm and dew-pearly,
Wakeful and starry:
Such fruits as these
No man can carry;
Half their bloom would fly,
Half their dew would dry,
Half their flavour would pass by.
Sit down and feast with us,   380
Be welcome guest with us,
Cheer you and rest with us.'—
'Thank you,' said Lizzie: 'But one waits
At home alone for me:
So without further parleying,
If you will not sell me any
Of your fruits though much and many,
Give me back my silver penny
I tossed you for a fee.'—
They began to scratch their pates,   390
No longer wagging, purring,
But visibly demurring,
Grunting and snarling.
One called her proud,
Cross-grained, uncivil;
Their tones waxed loud,
Their looks were evil.
Lashing their tails
They trod and hustled her,
Elbowed and jostled her,   400
Clawed with their nails,
Barking, mewing, hissing, mocking,
Tore her gown and soiled her stocking,
Twitched her hair out by the roots,
Stamped upon her tender feet,
Held her hands and squeezed their fruits
Against her mouth to make her eat.

   White and golden Lizzie stood,
Like a lily in a flood,—

Like a rock of blue-veined stone   410
Lashed by tides obstreperously,—
Like a beacon left alone
In a hoary roaring sea,
Sending up a golden fire,—
Like a fruit-crowned orange-tree
White with blossoms honey-sweet
Sore beset by wasp and bee,—
Like a royal virgin town
Topped with gilded dome and spire
Close beleaguered by a fleet   420
Mad to tug her standard down.

   One may lead a horse to water,
Twenty cannot make him drink.
Though the goblins cuffed and caught her,
Coaxed and fought her,
Bullied and besought her,
Scratched her, pinched her black as ink,
Kicked and knocked her,
Mauled and mocked her,
Lizzie uttered not a word;   430
Would not open lip from lip
Lest they should cram a mouthful in:
But laughed in heart to feel the drip
Of juice that syrupped all her face,
And lodged in dimples of her chin,
And streaked her neck which quaked like curd.
At last the evil people,
Worn out by her resistance,
Flung back her penny, kicked their fruit
Along whichever road they took,   440
Not leaving root or stone or shoot;
Some writhed into the ground,
Some dived into the brook
With ring and ripple,
Some scudded on the gale without a sound,
Some vanished in the distance.

   In a smart, ache, tingle,
Lizzie went her way;
Knew not was it night or day;
Sprang up the bank, tore thro' the furze,   450
Threaded copse and dingle,
And heard her penny jingle
Bouncing in her purse,—
Its bounce was music to her ear.
She ran and ran

As if she feared some goblin man
Dogged her with gibe or curse
Or something worse:
But not one goblin skurried after,
Nor was she pricked by fear;   460
The kind heart made her windy-paced
That urged her home quite out of breath with haste
And inward laughter.

  She cried 'Laura,' up the garden,
'Did you miss me?
Come and kiss me.
Never mind my bruises,
Hug me, kiss me, suck my juices
Squeezed from goblin fruits for you,
Goblin pulp and goblin dew.   470
Eat me, drink me, love me;
Laura, make much of me:
For your sake I have braved the glen
And had to do with goblin merchant men.'

  Laura started from her chair,
Flung her arms up in the air,
Clutched her hair:
'Lizzie, Lizzie, have you tasted
For my sake the fruit forbidden?
Must your light like mine be hidden,   480
Your young life like mine be wasted,
Undone in mine undoing,
And ruined in my ruin,
Thirsty, cankered, goblin-ridden?'—
She clung about her sister,
Kissed and kissed and kissed her:
Tears once again
Refreshed her shrunken eyes,
Dropping like rain
After long sultry drouth;   490
Shaking with aguish fear, and pain,
She kissed and kissed her with a hungry mouth.

  Her lips began to scorch,
That juice was wormwood to her tongue,
She loathed the feast:
Writhing as one possessed she leaped and sung,
Rent all her robe, and wrung
Her hands in lamentable haste,
And beat her breast.
Her locks streamed like the torch   500

Borne by a racer at full speed,
Or like the mane of horses in their flight,
Or like an eagle when she stems the light
Straight toward the sun,
Or like a caged thing freed,
Or like a flying flag when armies run.

   Swift fire spread through her veins, knocked at her heart,
Met the fire smouldering there
And overbore its lesser flame;
She gorged on bitterness without a name: 510
Ah! fool, to choose such part
Of soul-consuming care!
Sense failed in the mortal strife:
Like the watch-tower of a town
Which an earthquake shatters down,
Like a lightning-stricken mast,
Like a wind-uprooted tree
Spun about,
Like a foam-topped waterspout
Cast down headlong in the sea,   520
She fell at last;
Pleasure past and anguish past,
Is it death or is it life?

   Life out of death.
That night long Lizzie watched by her,
Counted her pulse's flagging stir,
Felt for her breath,
Held water to her lips, and cooled her face
With tears and fanning leaves:
But when the first birds chirped about their eaves, 530
And early reapers plodded to the place
Of golden sheaves,
And dew-wet grass
Bowed in the morning winds so brisk to pass,
And new buds with new day
Opened of cup-like lilies on the stream,
Laura awoke as from a dream,
Laughed in the innocent old way,
Hugged Lizzie but not twice or thrice;
Her gleaming locks showed not one thread of grey, 540
Her breath was sweet as May
And light danced in her eyes.

   Days, weeks, months, years
Afterwards, when both were wives
With children of their own;

Their mother-hearts beset with fears,
Their lives bound up in tender lives;
Laura would call the little ones
And tell them of her early prime,
Those pleasant days long gone   550
Of not-returning time:
Would talk about the haunted glen,
The wicked, quaint fruit-merchant men,
Their fruits like honey to the throat
But poison in the blood;
(Men sell not such in any town:)
Would tell them how her sister stood
In deadly peril to do her good,
And win the fiery antidote:
Then joining hands to little hands   560
Would bid them cling together,
'For there is no friend like a sister
In calm or stormy weather;
To cheer one on the tedious way,
To fetch one if one goes astray,
To lift one if one totters down,
To strengthen whilst one stands.'

GOBLIN MARKET (1862)

ANALYSIS

PART ONE LINES 1 TO 140

The sisters, Laura and Lizzie hear the cries of the goblin men selling their fruit. Laura is so tempted by their wares that she goes to them and, in exchange for a lock of her hair, she gorges on the fruit.

The narrative poem is written in an irregular rhyme scheme made up of loose iambic tetrameter which gives it a swift pace. This underlines the urgency of Laura's plight as well as the movement of the goblins through the glen.

The speaker of the poem is often assumed to be Laura, cautioning her children, but if this is so then she is self dramatizing. There seems to be a poetic voice which erupts in places.

The title of the poem suggests that the focus of the work is both the goblins and their market or world of financial exchange. This is important as the goblins seem to represent male society or sexuality, as well as the idea of a marriage market, or women as financial commodities.

The name Laura could be reminiscent of Petrarch's Laura to whom he wrote his sonnet cycle. In the sonnets she is a passive object of love, while here Rossetti makes her an active and sensual woman who seeks satisfaction. The name Lizzie could refer to Elizabeth I who had great phallic power and is seen as a dominant woman whose power rests in her unwillingness to lose her virginity.

The poem begins immediately with the threat of the goblins who can be heard by maids or virgins morning and evening. This means their temptation is ever present. The goblins shout "Come buy". It is important that they repeat this throughout. They are not offering free enjoyment; they want to solicit a contractual exchange in which they get something back from the maids. The fruits they offer are all ripe and perfect, yet they are from different parts of the world and are harvested at different times of year. This hints that their wares are not natural or wholesome. Some of the fruits are personified to emphasize the sense that they are sensual and bodily. The fruits are described as "sweet to tongue and sound to eye" – they feed the senses.

Laura "bows her head to hear", while Lizzie "veiled her blushes". They are both attracted to the goblins. Laura initially tries to resist, calling her sister to "Lie close" and "not look". Laura goes on to dwell on the origins of the fruit, wondering what "soil" cultivated "Their hungry thirsty roots?" These images are phallic, suggesting that it is a potent male sexuality which may come from a forbidden origin which she does not understand.

Throughout this section Laura's head is repeatedly described as "golden" and "glossy". This foreshadows the lock of hair she must exchange for the fruit. It also suggests her willingness as her head is constantly attracted to them. Is the emphasis on head also phallic, implying that Laura is aroused by the goblins?

Lizzie says their "gifts would harm us" and sticks her fingers in her ears, shuts her eyes and runs away. Therefore it is not that Lizzie is not aroused by them, it is just that she does not succumb.

Laura is curious and lingers. Sometimes curiosity is seen as a female sin, but it is important to note that Laura's own identification of the moral of the story is not something negative, but rather a positive belief in the importance of the sisterhood.

The goblins are repeatedly called merchants, so their selling is important. They are then described in animalistic terms as cats, rats, snails, wombats etc. Does this suggest that all men are bestial in their desires or that these goblins are a particular type of sexually threatening men?

Laura is described in a number of stanzas using lists of similes. These change throughout the poem. In line 81 Laura is like a swan, a lily, a branch and a vessel which has broken from its anchor. These images are both of purity, but also transgression.

When the goblins find her, their brotherhood is emphasized and the ways they are "leering at each other". They see her as a delight they can share. They display their fruit, but Laura has no money. Laura is very firm about not wanting to "purloin" their wares. She is afraid of being a thief. Therefore she is concerned to have a fair exchange with the men, but they are not honest merchants. They request a lock of hair. This is reminiscent of "The Rape of the Lock" by Alexander Pope in which the cutting of hair is symbolic of the loss of virginity. Laura cuts her own hair and weeps a tear "more rare than pearl". Pearl is usually symbolic of virginity. Then she "sucked their fruit globes". The image is deeply sexual. It seems to suggest fellatio, and the juice is sweet and strong. The verb to suck is repeated again and again. She is not described chewing or eating. This makes Laura appear out of control, child like or even sexually voracious. All she is left with is a kernel stone. Again this seems to be a testicular reference, or possibly a suggestion that the experience has hardened her. The stone is significantly inedible. She is left with nothing which will sate her. She leaves inebriated: "knew not was it night or day". The men disappear and she returns home.

PART TWO LINES 141 TO 319

Returning home, Laura is reminded of the tale of Jeanie by Lizzie. Jeanie ate the fruit and then wasted away and died. Laura begins to long for the goblin fruit, but unlike Lizzie she can no longer hear their cries and therefore cannot access what she needs. Instead she pines and dwindles.

Lizzie is waiting to meet Laura, admonishing her that "Twilight is not good for maidens." This suggests that as light diminishes virginity is threatened. She reminds Laura of Jeanie who after eating goblin fruit "pined and pined away" seeking them but never finding them again. She prematurely ages and dies. Her grave is infertile and no grass grows there or daisies. This suggests that Jeanie lost the opportunity of becoming a sexually fertile married woman because of her triste with the goblins.

Laura tells her sister that she ate but her mouth "waters still". These seem to be images of female sexual arousal. The experience has not sated her; it has created her appetite. She offers to bring Lizzie fruits the next day so she can be "done with sorrow". Therefore briefly Laura is happy. Together the sisters sleep "like two pigeons in one nest". Their unity is not diminished by Laura's intercourse with the goblins. They remain as close. Indeed the similes which describe them still refer to Laura like snow and ivory. These are images of virginity and purity. Does this mean that she has not lost her maidenhead, but has experienced a sexuality outside penetration, focussed on female pleasure? Even nature wants to ensure they have good sleep and so the owls avoid flying.

Next day the sisters do their work as usual, but Laura is longing for evening when she can return to the goblins. Note that their work and their home is significantly without men. They seem to live outside the patriarchy. Why is this a world without men? Why are the only male figures ravening goblins? However, when evening comes, Lizzie can hear the goblins, but Laura cannot. They go to collect water together. Water could represent washing something clean, but it is also an image of dripping arousal. Laura wants to linger, but Lizzie fears rain will "drench us through" or they might get "lost". Her fears are strange as surely these things have already happened to Laura? Laura is distraught that she cannot regain her pleasure. "Her tree of life drooped from the root." This is an image of detumescence. It appears Laura cannot find her sexual potency. It is odd that now the potency is described wholly in phallic terms. As she goes home, Laura's jug of water is "dripping all the way". This suggests that she is aroused but without an outlet for her desires. That night she weeps.

From then on Laura looks for the goblins, but cannot find them. Her hair grows grey and she starts to die. She desperately plants the stone kernel, but it will not grow. She has been blighted with sterility. Also she cannot create a "root" which again suggests her inability to arouse a phallus. Laura is imaged through a simile as a traveller in a desert who is thirsty but only sees mirages of oases. She stops doing her domestic jobs .

Lizzie wants to "share" her sister's pain, but is afraid "to pay too dear" – the image of financial exchange is here used to underline the terrible consequences transgression could inflict on a woman. Lizzie is reminded again of Jeanie who should "have been a bride; But who for joys brides hope to have Fell sick and died". This seems to say directly that it is Jeanie's enjoyment of sexual pleasure outside marriage which kills her.

PART THREE LINES 320 TO 446

Fearful Laura will die, Lizzie seeks the goblins and offers them a silver penny. However, they want her to eat in front of them and when she refuses they press the fruit on her. Lizzie keeps her lips sealed while she is attacked so nothing penetrates her. Frustrated with her, the goblins disappear after tossing back her silver coin.

When Lizzie realises Laura is close to death, she no longer worries about the risk to herself and putting a "silver penny" in her purse she seeks the goblins. In Elizabethan times a silver penny was slang for female genitalia. She goes to find the goblins.

The goblins laugh at her when they see her. They are described approaching her with a series of active verbs which show their enjoyment as well as their energy. They are often active in the poem, while women are conventionally passive.

Meeting Lizzie, the goblins immediately touch her. They describe their fruits using the possessive pronoun "our" which makes it sound like part of their body. They offer her an apple first, which reminds us of the Garden of Eden. At line 362 Lizzie appears to interrupt their sales talk. Instead she takes control of the transaction. She is active, not passive. She holds out her apron for them to fill and tosses them her penny. Interestingly, because she "tossed" the penny, she does not touch them. She remains intact and distant from them. She establishes a fair economic relationship, but the goblins do not like her contract. They want her to "eat with us". It is important that the goblin fruit is not really the location of their evil. What they want, in a prurient and voyeuristic way, is to watch the women eat the fruit. This suggests that they want to watch women taking pleasure. This must be an image of female masturbation and a reference to male pornography and exploitation of female self-pleasure. Pornography is also a financial transaction in which a woman's body is sold.

However, Lizzie breaks the transaction by ensuring it is she who pays and who refuses to pleasure herself in front of them. When the goblins refuse to sell her the fruit unless she eats with them, Lizzie demands her penny back. She is confident in her rights as a consumer. She is not to be exploited. At this point the goblins begin to abuse her. They start by calling her names and then they physically molest her. She is being attacked for not participating in the patriarchal game of women as objects of pleasure for men to exploit. However, as they abuse her they try to force the fruit into her mouth. Lizzie is described with a series of similes which liken her to a lily in a flood, a rock in a tide, a lighthouse in a storm, a fruit tree beset by wasps and a town besieged. Each image makes Lizzie powerful against assault. She is depicted as impervious. Many of the images are also quite phallic: the rock which is "blue-veined" and the "beacon" especially. Lizzie's reluctance to "open lip from lip" is a yonic image of her refusal to be penetrated by the men. Her mouth stands in for her vagina in the assault. She is covered by the juices of the fruit which "drip" and splash her face "like curd". This is an ejaculatory image; the fruit juices are semen. Weary with her resistance, the goblins fling "back her penny" and disappear, importantly "Not leaving root or stone or shoot". Each of these is a phallic image. So despite ejaculating over her, they have not satisfied their phallic desires.

PART FOUR LINES 447 TO 567

Lizzie delightedly returns to Laura and tells her to suck the fruit off her body. Now Laura hates the taste of the fruit, but having eaten it she goes through a kind of death, and in the morning she awakes well. Later the sisters are married and tell the story to their children, using it to teach the moral: there is no friend like a sister.

When Lizzie leaves her encounter, Rossetti repeats the line she "Knew not was it night or day". This suggests that although Lizzie has resisted their penetration, she has still taken pleasure from the event. Moreover, she has done so without paying for it; she returns with her penny intact. She runs home, not "pricked by fear". She is unafraid of the phallus.

At home, Lizzie calls Laura and tells her to kiss and suck the juices from her: "Eat me, drink me, love me". The image of love is again one of consumption, but this time Lizzie offers the contract for free. She gives her sister fruit not because she wants anything in return, but because she loves her. Initially, Laura is concerned for Lizzie, but she kisses and sucks away the fruit, but this time it is foul to her. She rips off her clothes and becomes active leaping around.

The poetic voice erupts into the poem with the pronouncement: "Ah! fool, to choose such part of soul-consuming care!" – this exclaims against Laura's gorging – this time on fruit which is bitter to her. "She fell at last". Laura falls. This could refer to her moral fall. She passes the night as if dead, but in the morning she awakes with her innocence returned to her. Her hair has gone from grey back to "gleaming". This could be a religious resurrection with Laura as a Christ figure.

The final stanza reassures us that the experience did not harm the sisters. They married and had children. Laura tells the "little ones" of the goblin men and how her sister saved her: "For there is no friend like a sister." Interestingly, the moral of the tale is not against transgression, but to approve the bravery and companionship provided by the sisterhood. It is a celebration of female solidarity and courage. The next generation learns this lesson.

TWICE

I took my heart in my hand
  (O my love, O my love),
I said: Let me fall or stand,
  Let me live or die,
But this once hear me speak—
  (O my love, O my love)—
Yet a woman's words are weak;
  You should speak, not I.

You took my heart in your hand
  With a friendly smile,   10
With a critical eye you scanned,
  Then set it down,
And said: It is still unripe,
  Better wait awhile;
Wait while the skylarks pipe,
  Till the corn grows brown.

As you set it down it broke—
  Broke, but I did not wince;
I smiled at the speech you spoke,
  At your judgement that I heard: 20
But I have not often smiled
  Since then, nor questioned since,
Nor cared for corn-flowers wild,
  Nor sung with the singing bird.

I take my heart in my hand,
  O my God, O my God,
My broken heart in my hand:
  Thou hast seen, judge Thou.
My hope was written on sand,
  O my God, O my God: 30
Now let thy judgement stand—
  Yea, judge me now.

This contemned of a man,
  This marred one heedless day,
This heart take Thou to scan
  Both within and without:
Refine with fire its gold,
  Purge thou its dross away—
Yea, hold it in Thy hold,
  Whence none can pluck it out.   40

I take my heart in my hand—
  I shall not die, but live—
Before Thy face I stand;
  I, for Thou callest such:
All that I have I bring,
  All that I am I give,
Smile Thou and I shall sing,
  But shall not question much.

TWICE 1864

ANALYSIS

The title refers to the act of offering her love which occurs twice with two different outcomes. The structure of the poem uses lots of repetitions to emphasize that the act has to be repeated because the male lover fails to accept her. The male lover is shown to be cruel (?) or careless with her emotion. Perhaps it is him who is not mature enough for love? The poem suggests that men are often to blame for relational difficulties even though traditionally much is blamed on women.

The poem opens with the female taking her heart out to give to him. The heart is a metaphor of love, but not just romantic love. It seems also to encompass spiritual love and love of oneself. The echoed voice saying "o my love" shows the depth of her passion for the man. She speaks to him for the first time "once hear me speak" to profess her love. Her bravery is underlined by her willingness to live or die. She concedes that conventionally it should be the man who speaks and not the woman because women's words are meant to be "weak", but clearly he has not spoken and has forced her to take the lead. Her bravery and unorthodoxy are not rewarded.

He takes her heart in a "friendly" way suggesting he does not love her, but may have misled her into loving him. He scans her heart with a "critical eye". This shows that he judges her. This is not a loving act. He discards her love by setting her heart down. He tells her she is too immature for love and is not ready. He employs natural metaphors of the heart as an unripe fruit and the necessity of waiting for harvest. His words could disguise his own unreadiness for love, or they could suggest that he does not understand or appreciate her, or that he is simply cruel in response to her love.

As he puts her heart down, he breaks it. She remains brave and does not flinch. Instead she smiles at his words. Her bravery and restraint is almost stereotypically masculine. Her self respect keeps her from letting him know the damage he has done. Since that time the many negative words show us that she does not smile or enjoy nature.

Once again, she gives her love. This time she gives her heart to God. She gives him her broken heart to make it good again. She asks him to judge her. Notice that she never asked for the man's judgement, but she got it anyway. She explains her "hope was written on sand". This metaphor shows that she knows her love was impermanent and could be easily obliterated by the tide.

She asks God to perfect or "refine" her broken heart and using a metaphor from metal smelting she asks him to use fire to take away the dross and keep the gold. This will undo what the "contemned" or scornful man has done to her. It will resolve the ruined day he made of her life.

Once God has helped her she can take back her heart and live again. She offers her love to God knowing he will "smile" to receive it. She concludes that she "shall not question much". Therefore has she become a more forthright woman than the one at the beginning who thought her words were "weak"?

WINTER: MY SECRET

I tell my secret? No indeed, not I:
Perhaps some day, who knows?
But not to-day; it froze, and blows, and snows,
And you're too curious: fie!
You want to hear it? well:
Only, my secret's mine, and I won't tell.

Or, after all, perhaps there's none:
Suppose there is no secret after all,
But only just my fun.
To-day's a nipping day, a biting day;
In which one wants a shawl,
A veil, a cloak, and other wraps:
I cannot ope to every one who taps,
And let the draughts come whistling through my hall;
Come bounding and surrounding me,
Come buffeting, astounding me,
Nipping and clipping through my wraps and all.
I wear my mask for warmth: who ever shows
His nose to Russian snows
To be pecked at by every wind that blows?
You would not peck? I thank you for good-will,
Believe, but leave that truth untested still.

Spring's an expansive time: yet I don't trust
March with its peck of dust,
Nor April with its rainbow-crowned brief showers,
Nor even May, whose flowers
One frost may wither through the sunless hours.

Perhaps some languid summer day,
When drowsy birds sing less and less,
And golden fruit is ripening to excess,
If there's not too much sun nor too much cloud,
And the warm wind is neither still nor loud,
Perhaps my secret I may say,
Or you may guess.

WINTER: MY SECRET

ANALYSIS

At the beginning of the poem, someone seems to have asked her to reveal her secret. The rest of the poem is a response to the request, saying she will not reveal it. There are lots of questions in the poem which could suggest the uncertainty of the speaker or simply emphasize the curiosity of the questioner. Note that Rossetti dwells on the perils of curiosity in other works.

The speaker uses the personal pronoun many times throughout the poem. This repetition of "I" underlines her strength of character and her strong sense of her own identity as something she wants to protect. She uses metaphors of the seasons to describe the trustworthiness of the world and whether or not she is therefore in a position to reveal the truth. Does this suggest that her world is unfriendly and cruel – it is winter and is too dangerous to venture into openly?

At the start of the second stanza she suggests that there may be no secret at all, and that she could be joking. In its manuscript form the poem was entitled "Nonsense". This might imply that there is no secret and that the focus of the poem is more about the relentless curiosity of the questioner.

She goes on to describe the current world as "nipping" and "biting". These personifications of the times are predatory and cruel, trying to consume her. She has to retreat into disguises with veils and cloaks and wraps. This hints that clothes or social conventions can be used to disguise and conceal the truth of a woman and that society does not allow women to reveal themselves fully. She imagines herself in doors, sheltering from the cold, where she will not open the door to any person who knocks. She describes a time of danger outside herself and the necessity to keep herself safely removed from others. She even compares the current world to the snowy wastes of Russia where people die from exposure. She refuses to test the good will of the questioner in case they wish to "peck" at her. Again the images are of consumption. She fears being eaten and destroyed if her secret emerges.

In the final two stanzas she looks at other seasons which might make it easier for her to reveal the secret. However, spring is not to be trusted as it is brief and its flowers can still be destroyed by a frost. Spring is imagined as vulnerable and ephemeral.

Finally she pictures summer, but her description is so specific it seems impossible. There must be "not too much" sun or cloud and a wind which is "neither still nor loud". This suggests there will never be a season appropriate for a woman to reveal her secrets; that the world will never be perfect for her.

SOEUR LOUISE DE LA MISÉRICORDE

I have desired, and I have been desired;
  But now the days are over of desire,
  Now dust and dying embers mock my fire;
Where is the hire for which my life was hired?
  Oh vanity of vanities, desire!

Longing and love, pangs of a perished pleasure,
  Longing and love, a disenkindled fire,
  And memory a bottomless gulf of mire,
And love a fount of tears outrunning measure;
  Oh vanity of vanities, desire!

Now from my heart, love's deathbed, trickles, trickles,
  Drop by drop slowly, drop by drop of fire,
  The dross of life, of love, of spent desire;
Alas, my rose of life gone all to prickles,--
  Oh vanity of vanities, desire!

[121]Oh vanity of vanities, desire;
  Stunting my hope which might have strained up higher,
  Turning my garden plot to barren mire;
Oh death-struck love, oh disenkindled fire,
  Oh vanity of vanities, desire!

SOEUR LOUISE DE LA MISÉRICORDE

ANALYSIS

The poem is set in the historical period of Jansenism which is an austere Catholic movement of the 17thC in France. The movement encouraged renunciation and living in religious orders. The speaker is a former royal mistress of Louis XIV (1661-1667) called Louise de la Valliere who has become a Carmelite nun to renounce her sins, called Sister Louise of Mercy. The poem is a dramatic monologue spoken in the voice of the nun called Louise. Despite being sequestered, the nun is tormented by desire and longing and this has wasted her life.

The stanza opens suggesting that she has both desired and been desired. This implies that she has had sexual and passionate experiences; she has had a full sexual experience. Her days of desire have been ended by becoming a nun, but ironically she is clearly still full of the emotion of desire even though she has been removed from it. She uses the metaphor of a fire for her desire. The word is repeated in every stanza to reiterate the inescapable nature of her longing. Her aging body is described as "dust and dying embers" which laugh at her desire. The persistence of her desire is ridiculous because she is too old and too locked away to enjoy it. The image of "dust" is reminiscent of the funeral service, suggesting that she is near the end of her life. She wonders what payment or recompense "hire" she has had for the life she has lived.

Each stanza ends with an exclamation "Oh vanity of vanities, desire!" This is an outpouring of emotion which rails against the desire she cannot stop feeling. The line alludes to Ecclesiastes from the OT "vanity of vanities, all is vanity" which says that all human endeavours are pointless. This line is a refrain, showing she cannot escape the emotion.

She juxtaposes the long vowel sounds of "Longing and love" with the crisp alliteration of "perished pleasure" to show how quickly her love has been destroyed. She creates the neologism "disenkindled" to show that her fire was once alive and has now been undone. The word "kin" is also hinted at which implies that due to her religious life she has been denied her family and children. She had five children by the king, but was tortured by her conscience all the time. The word "mire" is repeated to show that her memories cannot escape from the muddiness of her remembrances of passion. Her emotions are hyperbolically expressed. Her love has become a fountain of tears perpetually overflowing. There is no end to her passion and misery.

"Now" brings the reader back to her present misery. Her heart is dying. The stanza suggests post coital penises. The trickling could be ejaculation, while the idea of "spent desire" implies that her sexual experience has happened and left her bereft. Another phallic image is evident in the "prickles" of the rose that her life has become. Her life in a nunnery has destroyed her because it has thwarted her desire and made her unhappy.

Finally, she laments that her desire has prevented her from attaining a greater relationship with God. This is imaged through the metaphor of her garden turning to sterile mud. The phrase "death-struck" plays on the expected phrase "love-struck" to show that her life has been blighted by something deadly instead of life-giving. The fact she ends on the same exclamation shows that her thoughts have not progressed since the beginning of the poem and thus she has failed to resolve her emotions. The end of the poem has the speaker still unhappy and trapped in the emotion of desire.

Printed in Great Britain
by Amazon

40638348R00031